GET SMART FAST:

A Handbook for Academic Success

by Sondra Geoffrion

Published by

R & E PUBLISHERS

P. O. BOX 2008

SARATOGA, CALIFORNIA 95070

Library of Congress Card Catalog Number
85-62681

I.S.B.N.
0-88247-749-8

Library of Congress Cataloging-in-Publication Data

Geoffrion, Sondra.
    Get smart fast.

    Summary: Discusses various methods of improving
study habits including setting goals and organizing a
schedule. Also describes techniques for writing
outlines and essays and preparing for tests.
    1. Study, Method of. 2. English language--
Composition and exercises. 3. Examinations--Study
guides. [1. Study, Method of. 2. English language--
Composition and exercises. 3. Examinations--Study
guides] I. Title.
LB1049.G45 1986   371.3'028'12   85-62681
ISBN 0-88247-749-8 (pbk.)

TABLE OF CONTENTS

       Analyzing your schedule
       General study considerations
       Scheduling study time
       Using a calendar and a daily log
       Illustrations of a daily log

       Setting specific reading goals
       Setting specific goals for math and factual courses
       Techniques to learn factual material
       When and how frequently to review
       Scheduling Review Time

LETTER
TO THE
READER

RIGHT NOW YOU CAN CHOOSE TO BE A MOST SUC-CESSFUL LEARNER AND A SCHOLAR! This book will show you how.

You have probably wondered why someone else seems to be more successful in school than you are. Probably your classmate studies the same material as you do but earns better grades because he or she uses different study techniques. That student simply knows "what" and "how" to study using methods that really work. You can too!

The word "study" really means the act or process of applying the mind to acquire knowledge. That process involves careful attention to, and critical examination of, a subject. The successful student is involved in the study process daily and knows that "study" is not a single activity. It is a complete series of organized activities. Those activities include scheduling and planning study time, outlining assignments and lectures, mastering the material, writing essays, preparing for quizzes and tests, and taking tests strategically to achieve good grades.

Your goal is to become a successful student so you can complete your education and succeed in a career of your choosing. It may sound absurd, but you could eat an elephant, if that was your goal. How would you do it? You would look it over, decide to tackle it piece-by-piece, determine a strategy, then attack it bit by bit. It wouldn't take long to learn how to eat it, and you would attain your goal.

Perhaps learning all the material presented in class and earning good grades seems like an impossible dream right now. The amount of material to be learned seems as immense as the size of an elephant. But, you can take control over your courses. You can improve your study habits. You can attack your courses from the first day of school on and even earn an "A" on the final exam.

This short book explores the complete study process. It will show you intelligent ways to simplify that process. You can make your study time very productive learning time. You will learn how to discover teachers' lesson plans and how to record and analyze the most important topics taught in the course. The book explains all about tests, how to prepare for them, and how to take them. After reading this book, you should immediately feel more comfortable about testing situations, and you should know how to make a test really work for you. Your efforts will be rewarded with higher grades in your courses.

Unfortunately, this is not a book for you to read quickly and put away. You will need to refer to it many times. Remember, if the "art of studying," and that is really what it is, was really easy, everybody would get excellent grades. Now this book will help you to improve your study techniques, catch up, or even surpass your classmates. You can be a super-efficient student with very little effort!

INTRODUCTION

This book is organized as a complete reference book to provide all students with the skills needed to succeed in the classroom and in career endeavors long after formal schooling has been completed. Its format and content have evolved over years of teaching, tutoring, and stressing study skills that reduce stress, promote success, build confidence, and raise students standards to levels higher than they have experienced before.

The ability to study and take tests efficiently is essential for academic survival. This book lays out the path to success. It is a concise guide to efficient studying and test-taking.

Section one, PLANNING FOR PRODUCTIVE STUDY TIME, demonstrates that the use of time involves scheduling studies and keeping records. A charted schedule includes at least one-half hour of study per course for each hour spent in class — PLUS time for review, travel time, work, sleep, meals, and pleasure. Record-keeping means using a calendar and writing a "daily log" to include assignment details, assignment topics, and class topics. The topic listing is a valuable tool for reviewing, determining study sessions, and studying for exams. Planning obviously prevents lost sleep, skipped meals, and the need for "cramming."

Section two, MAKING STUDY TIME PRODUCTIVE, sets specific study goals. Productive study methods introduced include:

setting specific goals before starting to study; surveying and discovering topics before reading or doing assignments, doing assignments topic by topic, analyzing and learning material, outlining; and summarizing. These methods assure concentration and mastery of each assignment.

Section three, WRITING EFFICIENT OUTLINES, provides necessary information about all aspects of efficient outlining. Frequently students write continuously during lectures and record verbatim from reading assignments. This chapter tells what information should be recorded and how to do it. The standard outline form is reviewed. Infrequently taught outline styles are explained, including: adding lecture notes to pre-written reading notes, writing lecture and outline notes on facing notebook pages, and recording lecture notes in reading margins. Attentive listening and intensive reading before writing are emphasized. When outlines are not reviewed and learned immediately, learning is postponed. Therefore, when and how to review material is fully explained. The importance of review to master material becomes meaningful to students.

Section four, WRITING EFFECTIVE ESSAYS, defines an essay and explains informational, descriptive, and explanatory essays. Teachers assume students understand how to read essay instructions or directions, and they want students to write effective essays that reveal knowledge and opinion about a subject. Instructions often are difficult for students. Therefore, essay vocabulary is stressed since it dictates the type of essay, how to write it, and what to include. Following the steps for writing essays, students will learn how to write a thesis statement that includes the topic and what will be said about it in the body of the essay. This section includes: how to organize information; how to limit a subject to control length; how to evaluate and form an opinion about a subject; how to develop the introduction, body, and conclusion; how to outline an essay; and how to revise a draft.

Section five, TYPES OF TESTS, explains each type of test and the instructional vocabulary used in teacher written and in standardized tests. Since students often misinterpret or fail to follow instructions, the chapter stresses the importance of following instructions.

Section six, PREPARING FOR TESTS, analyzes tasks needed to efficiently prepare for test taking. Teachers survey material to write exams: students should survey and analyze! This section explains that test preparation includes: advance planning for a thorough review; analysis of the course content, discovery of probable test questions, and recitation and mastery of information topic by topic. Students can detect if subject matter is relevant to informational, descriptive, or explanatory essays. They can and should write their own essay questions and prepare outlines for them. Finally, students learn that cramming can be eliminated by doing and learning assignments daily, reviewing the daily log, relearning forgotten information, and preparing for specific test questions.

Section seven, HOW TO TAKE TESTS STRATEGICALLY, explains that taking a test strategically involves reading the entire examination quickly for instructions, order of presentation, point value of the sections, internal clues, length, and overlapping or repeated questions, and then allowing time for each part of the test. The section gives tips for taking each type of test, lists words that limit responses or signal a true or false answer, provides steps for taking multiple choice tests, and reveals clues to look for in short answer and matching tests. More essay test writing tips are offered, including: planning an essay to answer a question, outlining an essay, writing briefly and clearly, using illustrative devices like underlined words and graphs, and submitting a complete paragraph style outline when time is critical. One-fifth of the time allotted to an essay should be for planning: four-fifths should be devoted to writing. Returned tests should be saved and analyzed to improve test taking skills.

Finally, section eight, CONCLUDING REMARKS FOR YOUR SUCCESSFUL FUTURE, develops five strategies directly

3

related to academic achievement: a determination to succeed; a basic complete study schedule adapted to meet all study requirements; the discovery of the teacher's lesson plan; a knowledge of test vocabulary, types of tests, and how to take tests; and a resolve to take control of your studies. Having learned and used the study skills in this book, a student can earn excellent grades with very little effort.

CHAPTER 1
Planning for
Productive
Study Time

A good study schedule faithfully adhered to becomes routine. Lost study time can become a thing of the past. Every moment devoted to studying can be so productive that maximum learning can occur.

An important key to success in life is using all of your time wisely and efficiently. Perhaps it never occurred to you to actually plan a study schedule. Certainly you do schedule appointments, social engagements, and meals. You allot time for those activities. You also need to plan and schedule just the right amount of time for studies.

Analyzing your present schedule

Think about your present schedule of activities and your study requirements. If you don't have enough time for your studies and end up cramming or staying up very late at night, you need to change your habits.

Start by making a large chart of all the hours in a week when you are awake. Include the weekend. Leave big spaces and pencil in each class hour, meal times, travel time, work hours, and regular activities. If you don't have any free time left, your first priority is to adjust activities so you have adequate time for studies.

General study considerations

Teachers generally assign one half hour of study and preparation for each hour you spend in class. That means that you should be studying at least two and a half hours each day if you have five classes each day. For classes that do not meet every day, plan ten to fifteen minutes of studying and review on the day the class meets plus a half hour before that class meets again. Your courses may already require more than a half hour each.

Most effective learning takes place when a day's work is still very fresh in your mind. Fifteen minutes to review and learn notes as soon as possible after class is fifteen minutes of valuable learning time.

Distribute your study time. Split two reading sessions with a writing or math study to avoid fatigue. Difficult or demanding courses, one with a lecture and a laboratory, or extensive reading courses will require more of your time. Plan for breaks and meals when you schedule your studies.

Plan in advance for research papers and lengthy assignments. Plan to schedule a few hours each week for review and test preparation. A weekly review in each course never hurts. It reinforces learning. Never leave an entire review until the day before an exam. Test preparation should always be spread out over several study sessions.

You should not have to ever forfeit sleep or meals. Your health is most important. With advance planning, you can always complete all that needs to be done.

Scheduling study time

Look at the chart you made. Go back to your class hours and write in ink the courses they represent. Put an asterisk on the hours you know you're alert and productive. Those will be your study hours.

Determine your study requirements for each of your courses. How much time does it take to prepare for each course? How long does it take you to learn assignments and do assignments? How long does it take you to learn class notes each day? Are you doing poorly in a class, not adequately preparing for it, not concentrating, or not studying the right material? Are you presently cramming for exams? Analyze your study habits very honestly.

Set a tentative study schedule for each course and pencil it in. Revise the chart until you feel comfortable about how you will spend your time. Check to see if you have allocated enough time or even a little too much. Have you actually set aside several hours for general reviews, test reviews, long assignments, and test preparation? Revise your plan until you are satisfied, and then try it for a week and make adjustments.

Put your chart up on the wall or someplace where you can readily refer to it several times a day. Commit yourself to your study times. The chart is the basis of your daily planning.

Using a calendar and a daily log

As you recall, your objective is to allocate just the right amount of study time for each course. Therefore, you have to know what you have to study, and then determine how much time it will take to accomplish it.

Use a calendar with big spaces to record homework, due dates, exam dates, and appointments. The calendar is not for the details of assignments. Those should be written completely in your class notebook.

The most efficient and valuable way to organize and record what you have to learn is to write a "daily log" which is a list of all homework assignments, class topics, and activities. On just a few pages, you have a record of every major topic presented in class. By daily recording topics, you have written the teacher's complete lesson plan by the end of the course. The list is invaluable for review purposes.

The daily log is kept separately from the class notes. Begin with the last page in your class notebook using the book in reverse. In the left column, record homework assignments. Enter the date assigned, due date, the entire assignment, and particular instructions. If you know the assignment topics, list them. If not, go back and fill in the topics when you do the homework. Include in that same column announced test dates and the material to be included in the test.

In the right column of the daily log, record topics covered in class every day. Very briefly indicate the topics the teacher presented. One or two words will probably be adequate for each topic. If you had a class activity, write in what you did and why that was important. Focus on what the teacher emphasized. This is your method of recording the teacher's lesson plan.

The daily log is so simple and so much easier to review very quickly than finding main topics in your class notes. It is extremely valuable for exam reviews. When you review for a quiz, test, or final, you can instantly see how many hours were spent on one topic and which topics were less significant. You will know which topics you have forgotten. You will be able to see how the topics relate to each other. You will be able to plan your review studies much more easily.

The following illustration indicates the value of a topic listing separate from your notes. It presents a quick review for study and test preparation purposes. It is efficient and conserves your valuable time.

Illustrations of a daily log

Note how easy it is to read across the page. You can immediately see the relationship of the assignment to the class work.

English class log

Assignments

Oct. 6 -due- Oct. 7
read Act 1, Anthony and Cleopatra
pg. 109

Oct. 7 -due- Oct. 8
read Act 2
briefly analyze characters:
  Mark Anthony, Cleopatra,
  Octavius Caesar

Classwork

Oct. 7
discussed Act 1
Shakespeare: how he portrays
  scenes
  Scene 1, changes/why?
Oct. 8
Discussed Act 2
Discussed characters: Mark
  Anthony, Cleopatra, Eno-
  barus (his character, relationship to Mark Anthony
  and Cleopatra)
Note: (Octavious Caesar not
discussed in class - may be
essay question)

Math class log

Assignments

Oct. 1 -due- Oct. 3
read decimals pgs 175-177
know: what they are and
when to use them (6 uses)

Oct. 3 -due- Oct. 4
problems pg. 180, Nos. 9-18
when to use decimals
quiz on Oct. 6
  decimals: what are they,
  when to use, changing
  decimals to fractions

Classwork

Oct. 3
Decimals: definition
  reading decimals in class
  changing decimals to fractions
Board work: pg. 180, Nos. 3,
  7, 8
Oct. 4
Decimals: addition of. pg. 181

You now know an efficient way to record topics and assignments. The trick really is making every study minute a very productive one. How is that possible? Read on. The next chapter could be a turning point in your academic endeavors.

CHAPTER 2
Making Study Time Productive

A few minutes of studying can be more effective than several hours if you first set specific subject related study goals. Study with a purpose!

No matter how much time you devote to your studies, it must be used productively. Real learning and a sense of satisfaction must result. Teachers and good students know this. Few of them actually reveal their own effective study techniques so this chapter will help you.

In class, teachers quickly give assignments. They say "read," "do problems. . . ," "answer questions. . . ," or the like. Fortunately, key unspoken words like "learn," "know," "relate," "analyze," "memorize," and "understand" are omitted from the brief instructions. However, teachers assign material to be learned totally.

The way you start to accomplish your assignments makes the difference between learning and not-really-learning the contents. A "whip it out" or "get it done quickly" attitude simply is not an efficient use of your time and energy if you don't actually learn the contents totally. Simply reading an assignment from the first word to the last and closing the book does not mean you have totally comprehended what you have read. Doing problems mechanically does not assure content knowledge either. You must really learn everything possible in every assignment.

Productive study time involves starting every study session with very specific study goals or objectives. You must decide what the content of the assignment is, and then learn it the very first time you encounter it. If you don't learn it the first time, you merely postpone that learning session until some future time. Cramming for exams may result. There are definite ways, however, to learn and retain knowledge every time you do an assignment.

Setting specific reading goals

Specific study objectives must relate to the topics you are studying. Therefore, you must determine the topic or topics of the assignment before you begin the study. For reading assignments, reading a chapter is not a specific study objective. If you simply read, you won't remember much of the content when the book is closed. Three steps are involved to maximize your learning.

> *Survey to determine specific reading goals*
>   *— pre-read*
>   *— make up questions to set reading objectives*
> *Read the assignment topic by topic*
>   *— analyze each topic*
>   *— outline each topic*
> *Review and learn the entire assignment immediately*

1.   Survey to determine specific reading goals

Skim the chapter and pre-read it. First read the title, then the headings. Now read sub-headings, summary statements, and the closing paragraphs. If there are questions at the end of the chapter, read those as well. Search for as many of the main topics as possible plus a sense of the material. You may find it helpful to list them on a piece of paper. This step only takes you a couple of minutes, but you gain a roadmap to your reading.

After you have discovered the topics, you are ready to make up questions that will serve as guideposts when you read the material. Make up questions that ask "who," "why," "when," or "to what extent." Simply turn statements into questions. As you begin to read, you will actively search for the answers to your questions. You will know when you have read a complete main topic. You will find yourself really concentrating on the contents.

2. Read the assignment topic by topic

Read the entire first main topic. Read for a total understanding of that main topic, discovering all the sub-topics and the related facts. Search for the answers to your questions. Stop frequently to organize your thoughts and to review what you have read.

Perhaps you underline or highlight your book as you read. That is fine, but go one step further. When you have completed a topic, make up a question for every underlined sentence to extract the details from each paragraph. Be sure you can answer your questions.

Analyze the first topic you read. Discover the relationship of the sub-topics to the main topic. Discover possible test questions, facts, ideas, and the relationships presented. Know what examples you can give as supporting evidence to statements. Recite the material to yourself.

You have gone through the discovery process. Once you know the importance of the first main topic, it is opportune to write a brief outline to clearly show that topic. That provides you with an instant review later. You won't have to review your underlined book or read it again. Do the rest of the assignment topic by topic: reading; analyzing and learning; and outlining.

3. Review and learn the entire assignment immediately

More time should be spent actually learning the assignment than is allowed for reading and outlining! Go over the particulars mentally. Memorize. Keep reciting until you have mastered the contents. You should be able to relate your new knowledge to someone else before you put the assignment aside.

Setting study goals for math and factual courses

Naturally some courses don't involve much reading. Math is one. Others are sciences, foreign languages, and even accounting. They are all taught in a very specific sequence. Facts and material presented in class one day supplement and build on previous work. Mastering classwork and assignments on a daily basis is the key to success.

Simply being able to do math problems isn't enough. There is always some memorization of the step-by-step procedure to solve problems. You must know the concepts and the vocabulary of the course.

Specific study objectives for factual courses involve understanding the concepts, memorizing them, doing the assignment, and analyzing it. The steps are similar to those for reading assignments. They are:

Survey and set specific goals
  — discover the concepts or vocabulary
  — memorize those first
Do the assignment and check your work
Analyze the assignment
Review and recite immediately

1. **Survey and set specific study goals**

   Pre-read the assignment. Look for concepts in math. Find the new vocabulary in all subjects. Discover what the whole assignment involves.

   Naturally you should read the text even if your assignment is merely to do a few problems. Teachers highlight and illustrate, but texts often explain material more thoroughly and sometimes even better than the teachers do. Exam questions often are directly from the text. Reading the book is very important.

   Learn the concepts and the vocabulary of the assignment. You must eventually learn them anyway. It is best to do it before you do the assignment. You will then be reviewing and using your information when you do the assignment.

2. **Do the assignment and check your work**

   The assignment is your method of determining if you have actually learned the concepts, formulas, and vocabulary. Refer back to the text if necessary. Check your work very, very carefully.

3. **Analyze the assignment**

   This is an important step. Specifically note if there was any variation in the problems you have done. Perhaps some were a little harder or some had you apply a concept in a slightly different manner.

   A math problem is only a statement with an unknown. Try to discover ways you could write a different problem by varying the unknown. For languages, try using the vocabulary you just learned in various sentences. Always try to apply your new knowledge in a different way. Apply it to the classwork as well.

4. Review and recite

Learn the concepts and the terminology so well that you can teach someone else. You might want to write notes for review purposes. You could eliminate the need to return to the text for any reviews. Your review and learning, and possibly note-writing, will prepare you for any possible unannounced quiz. You will have learned the material and will remember it.

Techniques for learning factual material

Self-testing devices are always helpful in learning facts. To master long lists, you could try a divided piece of paper with a word to be defined in one column and its definition in another. You could use this method for dates, names, spellings, descriptions, vocabulary, scientific terms, etc. Fold the paper back to test yourself.

Another device is a tape recorder if you have one available. Record the fact to be learned, leave a blank space while saying the definition to yourself, then record the definition. Play it back and test your ability to supply the definition before you hear it spoken.

The best device for remembering a list of topics or items in a series usually is to write the list so you can visualize it on a page. You could then make up a nonsense word consisting of the first letter of each item in order. If you can remember that nonsense word, you won't leave out any item in the list. You could also try to remember items by associating them to something else or by learning how many items are in the list.

Memorization should be done in short, concentrated study sessions. Decide what you must learn, memorize, visualize it with your eyes closed, then check your list for accuracy. You may have to learn it again. Find a method that works for you. After a memorization session, do something else, then re-check to see if you remember everything accurately.

Scheduling Review Time

Plan the first review immediately after you have studied. Recall the important points in a chapter, the vocabulary you just learned, and the concepts that were new. Check yourself to see if you have included all the important facts. Be able to relate your new knowledge thoroughly to someone else.

Plan one or two reviews before the exam review. Actually, a weekly review in each subject is even better. Concentrate on re-learning. That will necessitate reviewing your daily log, reading your notes, reviewing the text, and re-learning forgotten facts.

Ideal exam reviews concentrate on recitation, not learning. There will be some re-learning necessitated as you review the important topics and get right to the heart of a course. While you were doing daily assignments, reviewing class notes, and learning both, you were also pinpointing possible and probable test questions. Therefore, test reviews concentrate on reciting all the material, relating the topics to each other, and learning the answers to the questions you know will be asked on the exam. Chapters five and six will help you for exam reviews.

You have just read the simple process of making study time most productive and efficient. This is the only approach to any assignment that assures maximum opportunity for learning. It enables you to retain your knowledge and apply it in the classroom. You will be learning the material in each assignment every day. Cramming will not be necessary.

Try the methods suggested in this chapter. You will most definitely see improvement in your learning, retention, and application of knowledge.

CHAPTER 3
Writing
Effective
Outlines

Carefully constructed class and reading outlines are the most valuable learning tool. They are far more efficient than highlighted books or tape recordings.

A lecture is quickly forgotten, and a book contains lots of unimportant information. You can record the relevant information of a whole text or lecture on just a few sheets of paper. Brief outlines are effective and vital for review and learning purposes.

Outlines are more efficient than tape recordings. Only a portion of a lecture contains information for you to learn. Why tape record a whole lecture, then listen to it again, since you can extract the facts in class?

Outlines are more efficient than underlined or highlighted books. Outlines don't complicate learning. They clearly show the inter-relationship of topics to sub-topics. They are a paraphrase and intentionally eliminate all extraneous words or ideas.

Outlines are concise time-savers. It takes more time to learn and review from a marked book or a tape than it takes to read an outline. You don't need to waste time pondering underlined sentences, analyzing them, and skimming for related sub-topics to collect information to learn. If you must return to an underlined book for each review, you will be repeating the process several times during the term. Outline instead or in addition to underlining.

Information you need to record

Have you ever stopped to think of a list of things you will be tested on? Have you then thought about how you might be asked to use the information on a test? The following list may help you locate some of the important information in your courses.

> *You will need to know:*
> *—factual information to prove or support an idea*
> *—causes and effects*
> *—names, titles, authors, dates, and the like*
> *—theories, their interpretation, their importance and impact on history, society, or other events*
> *—descriptions of people or characters and their relationship to others*
> *—critical evaluations stating your opinions and judgment with reasons to support your beliefs*

Don't panic! There is nothing on that list you don't already know. You can record all the necessary information, simplifying and condensing it to make the learning task as easy as possible for yourself.

Standard outline method

The most efficient notes are recorded with wide margins for later additions. Main topics are begun toward the left margin. These are well-phrased, meaningful statements. Secondary ideas, sub-topics, facts to substantiate the main topic, and illustrations are indented and written under the main topic. Further indentions may be necessary for additional examples.

Roman numerals (I, II, III. . .) are used for main topics. Capital letters (A, B, C. . .) are for sub-topics and Arabic numerals (1, 2, 3. . .) for facts and illustrations under the sub-topics. Use lower case letters (a, b, c. . .) and numbers in parenthesis (1) if further indentions are needed.

For example:

I. A daily log is a listing of topics, class activities, and assignments.
   A. The log is part of, but not a substitute for, class notes.
   B. It is a listing of classwork and homework.
      1. Write classwork in one column.
         a. the date
         b. major topics covered
         c. type of class activity performed
            (1) experiment number, etc.
      2. Write homework in the other column.
         a. date assigned
         b. assignment and detailed instructions
         c. test dates, type of test, what will be on the test
         d. topics covered in the homework
         e. assignment due dates

Outlining techniques that you can adapt

Once you are used to this formal method, it can be simplified slightly. You can omit the letters as long as you still indent and clearly show the main topic and sub-topics. You can develop your own style for efficiency in your notes.

You might want to record reading notes on only the left pages and lecture notes on the right pages. Outlines on the same topic can be arranged directly across from each other in the opened notebook. Repetition of the same material in two sets of notes can be avoided.

You might try leaving empty lines in your reading outlines to add lecture notes on the same topic in a different pen in class. If a teacher jumps from topic to topic, lecture notes could be entered in wide margins instead.

Outlining the reading assignment and adding to it in class almost always guarantees excellent notes. It is definitely a process to master. You have more time in class to actually listen to what is being presented and you will be writing less.

Outline reading assignments

If you merely start reading an assignment, find something you "think" is important, and write notes, the outline may not fully develop a topic. Your notes may not flow well. Reading and analyzing the material should precede notewriting.

Outlining is simplified by listing the main topics on scrap paper when you pre-read the assignment. Reading in blocks enables you to organize your outline topic by topic. You will paraphrase more and quote less.

Most authors use headings liberally. Not all of them will be major topics. Sometimes headings alone, or several combined, become a brief outline. Do write them as complete sentences.

Include terms and definitions in your outlines. Sometimes the definition is the main idea. Underline words you must learn and clearly define them.

Frequently you will recognize possible test questions when you do the reading. Include them in your notes, perhaps designating them with (T.Q.). They will be there for reviews.

Write summaries when you review the notes. Summarize the notes in fifty words or less. This process is burning the information into your memory. It gives you the ability to relate what you have learned if you are called upon in class. You can also check yourself for accuracy.

The importance of class notes

Listening to lectures and taking notes can really be very difficult for some students. Those who are afraid that they are going to miss something important write continuously. The notes may be verbose and meaningless. Time must be spent to edit and rewrite them.

Other students might omit notes entirely. They feel the presentation is clear and obvious so they will remember the lecture. Without some notes, they won't remember that class at all.

Lectures are not a substitute for reading the text. A lecture that follows a reading will simply reinforce your knowledge and supplement that reading. If you have done the reading and outlined it, your notes may simply be a list of topics presented in class, plus some additional notes.

Teachers survey a lot of material and give you a capsule version in class. Listen to the teacher's presentation, the sequence, and explanations. Note what is illustrated on the blackboard. You want to condense all of it in your notes.

Class outlines

You should spend more time listening in class than writing! Listen attentively for the main topic and the interrelated sub-topics. Paraphrase as much as possible. Write selectively and briefly after a whole topic has been presented. Be certain to include:

— terminology, definitions, correct spellings
— direct quotes in quotation marks
— blackboard illustrations and notes
— references to the text and readings
— possible test questions you hear in class

Your note writing style may vary from class to class depending on the teacher's style. Outline form may not actually work for you at all in some classes. However, disorganized notes are better than no notes — they can be revised and organized later. Too many notes are better than too few — they can be edited later.

Reviewing class notes

Re-read your notes as soon as possible after a class. Check the content of each topic for completeness and accuracy. You may need to re-write the notes quickly. You might want to underline key words that you will have to learn. You could make a reference to the text or to other notes. Make the notes complete and easy to learn.

Learn your notes immediately and write summaries. Now, write down possible test questions. Your questions will probably appear on an exam. A list of questions prepared after reviewing and learning notes is extremely helpful for review purposes. Make your notes the concise time-savers they are intended to be.

CHAPTER 4
Writing
Effective
Essays

Essays are the ultimate test of a writer's ability to interpret and explain a subject.

What is an essay?

An essay is a short composition about a single subject. It generally states a point of view. A well developed essay has three parts:

- —an introduction that presents the writer's thesis or subject and what will be said about that subject,
- —a body that develops that thesis and supports each part of it, and
- —a conclusion that summarizes the ideas and briefly explains their significance.

Three types of essays — informational, descriptive, and explanatory

There are three distinctively different types of essays. This chapter will clearly show you the differences and the instructional terminology for essays.

Informational essays reveal the facts the writer knows about a subject.

Descriptive essays convey the writer's dominant impression about a subject.

Explanatory essays tell what the writer thinks about a subject and why he things that way.

As you read the next few pages, it will become clear to you that whenever a teacher announces an essay assignment, record the instructional words verbatim. If the instructions are written on a test, the terminology used dictates the type of essay you will write.

Informational essay vocabulary

The purpose of the informational essay is to reveal facts and particulars about a subject. The teacher, therefore, is looking for an essay revealing your knowledge about specific material related very precisely.

The teacher's instructions that dictate an informational essay are listed here with a brief description of their meanings for all essay writing purposes. Totally familiarize yourself with this vocabulary list.

tell. . . *narrate* *enumerate* *list* *relate* *name* *recall* *state* *identify*	These words require the writer to give an account of, to list or name, in order, if necessary, without any further elaboration. The instructions may tell you to do something else with the list afterwards.
quote. . .	Repeat a passage verbatim.
cite. . .	Give examples, quote, give proof of, an explanation of, *or* name a person, place or thing.

define. . . State the precise meaning showing any and all distinguishing characteristics.

explain. . . Clarify, show how something functions, *or* interpret and give reasons for your interpretation.

expand. . . Develop an idea or topic with facts and details—include examples, if they are necessary.

classify. . .
rank
trace
organize
For all of these terms, outline in essay form, write a list, arrange a grouping—in order, if necessary.

tell. . . This can mean the same as narrate, list, and enumerate, *or* it can mean to relate in order, to express in words, to give an account of, or to state evidence.

evaluate. . . Appraise and describe the value or worth of the subject.

Descriptive essay vocabulary

Descriptive essays state the subject of the paper and give several broad categories or elements characteristic of that subject. Carefully note the terminology the teacher uses to indicate this type of essay.

characterize. . . Describe in detail, particular qualities, features, or traits of a person or group.

describe. . . Tell about the subject giving a very detailed account.

compare. . . Describe and examine the qualities or charac-

27

teristics of each subject *and* show the similarities and/or differences.

contrast... These words mean the same as compare *but*
differentiate show only the dissimilarities or differences.

sketch... In paragraph form, outline or describe the subject briefly, or design a graph if one is appropriate to the subject. "Sketch" does not mean to draw a picture.

summarize... Outline in paragraph form.

Explanatory essay vocabulary

Explanatory essays state what you, as the writer, think about a subject *and why* you think that way. Sometimes it is even necessary to state how you arrived at your opinion including the evaluative criteria you used to form your judgment.

Carefully note the terminology used and the differences between the following words. As you read this list, realize that any of the words that appeared on the informational essay list and the descriptive essay list can be used with the words on this list. Combined in any manner, you will have to write a two-part essay.

analyze... Break down a subject or idea into its various
explain parts, then give your opinion, *and* draw some
interpret conclusion, or state why you arrived at your opinion.

criticize... Analyze and examine a subject, give your judgment or opinion, *and* tell why you arrived at that opinion based on evidence you supply.

argue... Examine a subject from all angles, clarify and
discuss prove, state evidence and reasons for and/or

| *dispute* | against, *and* give reasons for your opinion. |
| *debate* | |

explain. . .	State the meaning or interpretation very
clarify	clearly and give reasons why the examples
exemplify	you cite apply. Give several examples or
how	comparisons *and* your opinion.
interpret	

| *synthesize. . .* | Present a total idea by explaining its parts and then integrating all the parts of the subject. In philosophy, this means to arrive at deductive reasons moving from a simple thought to a complex idea, noting the principle and how it applies by stating the causes and effects. Conclusions and opinions must be clearly stated. |

Seven steps for writing essays

1. *State your purpose for writing.*
2. *Select the subject and limit it.*
3. *List examples and supporting evidence.*

    For informational and descriptive essays:
    —list examples, facts, data, or supporting evidence to explain the subject, *then*
    —search for common characteristics, categories, and evidence for the body of the essay.

    For explanatory essays:
    —formulate an opinion about a subject,
    —write statements to explain the topic and your opinion, *and*
    —write statements explaining how you arrived at that opinion.

4. *Write a thesis statement that clearly and precisely states the subject and what you are going to say about that sub-*

ject. Test the thesis statement.

5. *Outline the essay.*
6. *Write to follow the outline.*
7. *Revise the first draft.*

State your purpose for writing

Teachers use very precise word choice whenever they assign an essay. Generally they give you the topic. Assignments should be recorded verbatim. Your essay must fulfill the assignment instructions.

The assignment itself determines your specific purpose for writing. Your purpose may be to explain, criticize, present a new idea, etc. The purpose of the assignment will help you to write the essay and to define the thesis statement.

For example, your assignment could be to "evaluate" a subject. Your purpose for writing will be to determine its value or worth by stating its qualities or characteristics. If the instructions are to write a "criticism," you would state and discuss the evidence about the subject for and against, giving your opinion. If the essay is an "interpretation and proof," your purpose is to explain the subject, giving evidence to conclusively prove your interpretation, then state facts that can disprove any contradictory statements.

Teacher's instructions are most important! They tell you explicitly what type of essay you are expected to write and even dictate how you should develop the essay.

Determine and limit the subject

The purpose of the essay determines the length of the composition. The subject of your essay must be specific enough for the length of your intended essay. Note the following thoughts on limiting a topic.

too broad. . .	the computer industry
slightly narrowed. . .	the history of computers in industry
narrower. . . .	the history of the computer industry in the United States

narrow enough for a 2,000 word essay. . .

the growth of the computer industry in the United States

narrow enough for a 1,000 word essay. . .

the computer industry today

narrow enough for a 500 word essay. . .

the current use of computers in the classroom

List examples and evidence for informational and descriptive essays

For informational and descriptive essays, you need specific facts, precise vocabulary, and compact organization of your subject. List the examples, facts, data, or supporting evidence you think will explain your subject. The list does not necessarily have to be in any particular order at first. Next search for common characteristics, categories, or patterns in that list to arrange your supporting evidence for the thesis and the body of the essay. Note how the unorganized list of items below can easily be grouped into the four main headings after the list is completed.

Characteristics of a good bicyclist:

unsorted list:

stops at red lights

is visible at all times

is courteous to other cyclists

signals clearly

is courteous to pedestrians

adjusts gears and lubricates bike

keeps tires in good condition

drives at moderate speeds

is alert

drives only where permitted

is cautious

keeps brakes in good condition

is courteous to other drivers

main topics and sub-topics:

—assumes a courteous attitude

(is courteous to pedestrians, cyclists, drivers)

—obeys the laws

(stops at red lights, signals clearly, drives only where permitted)

—drives carefully

(is alert, cautious, visible at all times)

—maintains the bicycle in good condition

(keeps the brakes and tires in good condition, and adjusts gears and lubricates the bike)

Evaluate and form an opinion about a subject for explanatory essays

For explanatory essays, it is necessary for you to state your opinion about the subject. You must support that opinion with examples, evidence, and facts. Your own judgment of the subject is involved in this process.

Three steps are involved in anticipating writing an explanatory essay, especially a criticism or an evaluation. The steps are:

1. Express and write a statement of opinion and the subject,
2. Write statements explaining the subject and your opinion,
3. Write statements explaining how or why you arrived at that opinion.

Explanatory essays requiring you to "analyze," "review," "prove," or "demonstrate," all involve criticism and evaluation of your subject. They all require your opinion and why you have formed that opinion. Examples, evidence, and facts to support that opinion are all vital and need to be included.

Critical judgment is necessary for writing good explanatory essays. Criticism and evaluation, then discussion and analysis, are the art of intelligent appraisal of a subject. Often this process is not taught in classrooms.

Criticism is a verbally expressed act of evaluation and assessment. When you express an opinion or a preference, an acceptance or a rejection, you have reasons for your statements. If the reasons are then questioned, you would have to state the evidence you used to make your appraisal. This is the process of evaluating any subject when you have to write an explanatory essay.

Although the word "criticism," when applied to essay writing, may be new to you, criticism is not new at all. You are engaged in criticism daily. In an English class you might be asked, "Does 'Moby Dick' present a better character study than 'Jonathan Livingston Seagull'?" A tennis friend or a gym instructor might ask, "Isn't your swing a little too choppy today?" In a history class you might be asked, "Was Dulles wise in taking sides with Portugal at Geneva?" These questions ask for your opinion, your judgment, and evidence to support your statements. This is the domain of explanatory essays.

Whether you judge the merits of a book, appraise the soundness of a governmental policy, or merely state why you like ice cream, you are engaged in criticism. Criticism can praise as well as blame, can be positive or negative, for or against.

You could conceivably have an assignment or a test question that requires you to, "*compare and contrast* two quotes, *discuss and evaluate* the author's intent, and *explain* why you agree with one author more than the other." This is a difficult three-part question that involves criticism and judgment. How would you now go about answering it? Read the question again. Decide your strategy before you read the next paragraph.

For the above question, you would (1) evaluate and interpret each of the quotes. List comparative ideas. Arrange the lists to form a comparison. (2) Decide what each of the authors intended to say. Form an opinion about each of the author's meanings and write separate statements giving evidence to support your statements. (3) You would then decide which of the authors you agree with and list your reasons. All of your statements would directly relate to your course material. The essay would develop each of the written steps. You would have to outline your answer before even attempting to write the essay.

It is definitely impossible to write a good explanatory essay without weighing the merits of the subject, assessing all the available evidence, and passing judgment to come to your own conclusion. If your conclusion or opinion makes sense *and* you can substantiate it with reasons, you have the basis for an excellent essay.

Write a thesis statement

This step involves writing a generalization that is suitable for developing a thesis statement. A *generalization* is an interpretative statement that requires several pieces of information and evidence to support it. A generalization suitable for writing purposes is interpretive, analytical, or explanatory. That means, the generalization answers "why" and "how" questions, or divides the subject into its component parts.

A *thesis statement* is always a complete sentence. The subject of the sentence is the topic of your essay. The predicate of that sentence states two or more things you will say about that topic. A thesis statement can use the word "because" to introduce the predicate items.

A thesis statement is never a statement of simple fact. It is never a question. Frequently used ideas, cliches, or very meaningless statements are not suitable thesis statements.

Examples of generalizations suitable for essays

The dental profession demands four important qualities: intelligence, dedication, self-control, and an interest in people.
 – This sentence breaks the subject down into its component parts, each of which can be explained in the body of the essay.

An author reveals character through description, what the

character does, what he says, and what others say about him.
  − The predicate of this statement explains "how" the author reveals character.

The basic philosophy of the American judicial system resembles the American business philosophy: they both accept competition as a way of life, they establish and enforce rules, and they settle disputes between their competitors.
  − This predicate answers the question "why."

Note: Each of the above sentences requires analysis and interpretation of all available supporting evidence before the sentence can be written. The sentences limit the length of the essay. You can now apply all of this information to the essays you will write and even analyze essays you have written to see how they could be improved.

Examples of generalizations not suitable for essays
cliches:
   The press reveals the pulse of public opinion.
   War is hell!

broad statements:
   Shakespeare is noted for his characters, imagery, and staging devices.
   (You don't want to write a book!)

meaningless statements:
   This is a good novel because it is interesting.
   (What do "good" and "interesting" mean?)

general or vague statements:
   Teenagers are too irresponsible to have checking accounts, charge cards, and full banking privileges.
   (This opinion statement cannot be proven conclusively.)

Note: The thesis statement is the crux of the essay! Always check and test your statement before writing your essay. Ask yourself:

1. Is the statement a direct answer to the assignment or test questions?

2. Can you prove the statement by stating enough valid evidence and facts for each part of the predicate?

3. Have you included enough examples or evidence, or too many, for the intended length and purpose of your essay?

4. Is your opinion valid and can you justify it?

Outlining an essay

Plan a scheme for your essay before writing. Your essay will then flow from one thought to another, be concise, and develop the thesis. Consider paragraphing, topic sentences, connectives, the introduction, and the conclusion.

The introductory paragraph briefly discusses ideas relevant to your thesis. The thesis statement is the *last* sentence in the paragraph.

The body develops the ideas in the predicate of the thesis statement. State each idea as the topic sentence of a separate paragraph. Each topic sentence needs two or more ideas or examples to explain it, *or* none at all. Develop each of your paragraphs to supply facts, evidence, and details from the list you have organized before writing the thesis statement.

You can go back now to the example of limiting a subject, "the characteristics of a good bicyclist," to see how you could write an outline for that topic.

The conclusion is usually brief. It re-states the thesis statement by paraphrasing it or by summarizing the ideas presented. It discusses the implication of those ideas and may briefly suggest a broader significance. It states and substantiates your opinion for explanatory essays.

The outline is the skeleton of your paper. Unless you have to submit it, the outline can be very simple.

For example:

Introduction:
- title and author if you are writing a book
- information relevant to the subject
- thesis statement

Paragraph one:
- topic sentence contains the first idea from the predicate of the thesis statement
- examples or evidence to support that statement

Paragraph two:
- topic sentence contains the second idea from the predicate of the thesis statement
- examples or evidence to support that statement

Other paragraphs to completely develop each part of the thesis statement

Conclusion paragraph
- re-states the thesis or summarizes the predicate of that statement
- reveals your opinion and the basis for your opinion
- states broader implications, if applicable

Write to follow the outline

A good essay develops only one topic. Writing an essay from an outline prevents changing the subject and introducing new ideas that are not relevant to your pre-determined thesis statement. Follow your outline.

Revise a first draft

Critically read your essay. Look for:

1. logical organization
2. proper paragraph division
3. topic sentences for each paragraph
4. content of each paragraph
5. complete sentences
6. clear statements
7. correct punctuation
8. precise vocabulary
9. correct spelling
10. substantiated thoughts
11. a clear statement of your opinion

Conclusions

Analysis and evaluation of the subject matter presented in a course is crucial for essays. Your opinion, as well as the reasons for that opinion, reveal your knowledge and your assessment of the course material. If you can reveal your understanding and comprehension of material presented in class very coherently in an essay, the teacher will most certainly be impressed. The organization of an essay presented in this chapter will be very valuable for you to refer to frequently.

Now try to organize a short essay using perhaps a previous essay test question. Follow the procedure step-by-step until you are thoroughly familiar with the techniques. Learn the precise vocabulary used in essay instructions. Try writing thesis statements when you review your lecture notes. Specific tips about preparing for and taking the essay test are in the next three chapters. They, too, will help you.

CHAPTER 5
Types of
Tests

Learn as much as is possible about tests: their vocabulary, what they test, and how they do it. You should never be surprised or confused when you receive a test.

Test performance can be improved. You can do it! The key is to be able to follow instructions once you are in the test situation.

If you are one who tenses and panics whenever a test is announced, then forgets crammed information during the test, don't give up. This chapter will help you.

The information in this chapter will familiarize you with the various types of tests. Chapter six will help you prepare for tests. Chapter seven will give you several test-taking tips. You can make a test work for you! You will be able to reveal your knowledge without fear and apprehension.

All tests contain very specific vocabulary that instructs you and directs your responses. Have you noticed how very frequently teachers mention that some students do not follow instructions? Their grades suffer. An absolute knowledge of test vocabulary is the most important information you can master.

True-false tests

This test presents a statement and instructs you to decide whether it is true or false. The directions will tell you to write in "true" or "false," "T" or "F," "circle" the *correct* response, or "cross out" the *incorrect* response. Follow instructions!

Multiple choice tests

This type of test lists a number of answers designed to look alike, but only one is correct.

Multiple choice vocabulary tests direct you to either select a *synonym* (a word that has the same meaning as the stated word) or an *antonym* (a word that means the opposite of the given word).

Sequence multiple choice tests instruct you to put the choices given in their correct order, generally historical order.

Analogy tests require you to compare the relationship between two ideas or things to another set of ideas or things that have a very similar relationship.

Fill in short answer tests

These questions require you to write in a response.

The completion short answer test presents a statement that must be completed with one or more words that you will write in. Sometimes you must fill in the blanks or write in with no blank spaces clearly defined. You could have to write a word or words to complete a statement where the only clues may be the number of fill in lines, a singular or a plural verb, or an "a" or "an" preceding the writing spaces.

The number series fill in test states a series of numbers in correct order or sequence and you are required to supply the next number or two to complete the series or sequence.

Matching tests

This test consists of two lists placed side-by-side. You must select a response from one list that matches one from the other list, either by drawing lines or by numbering one list.

Cross out tests

This type is almost self-explanatory. You must cross out or eliminate the wrong item or response. The cross out test can be a two-part question if you have to then supply the correct answer.

Essay tests

Informational essay questions require you to write an essay that provides facts and very specific knowledge of a subject. The instructions will contain words such as tell, narrate, enumerate, list, relate, name, recall, state, identify, quote, cite, define, clarify, explain, expand, classify, rank, trace, organize, or evaluate.

Descriptive essay questions require you to state and define the subject and give characteristics or descriptions. The instructions will most likely include the words: characterize, describe, depict, compare, contrast, differentiate, sketch, or summarize.

Explanatory test questions direct you to tell what you know about a subject in good essay form *and* give your opinion about why you formed that opinion. Not all the questions state that your opinion is required, but it is. The instructions include words such as analyze, explain, interpret, criticize, argue, dispute, debate, explain, clarify, exemplify, interpret, and synthesize. Words from the other essay questions can appear as well.

Go back to the chapter on essays and really learn the essay terminology! You cannot possibly bluff your way through an essay test. Essays must fulfill the requirement of the instructions. Terminology and word meanings are vital for all essay test success.

CHAPTER 6
Preparing
for
Tests

The three simple secrets to achieving top grades on tests are: preparing thoroughly, discovering the test questions, and answering the questions directly.

Your first objective is to discover what material will be tested and what type of test you will have. Ask in class! Generally a teacher will give some guidelines regarding subject content and the type of test. Any information you can obtain will assist you to prepare.

Do a preliminary review and set study goals

Several days before the exam, re-discover the teacher's lesson plan and set specific study goals. If you keep a daily log, you merely have to review the list of topics covered in class and in the assignments.

If you only have a set of notes to review from, skim the notes and list major topics. Write in margins if necessary or use a separate sheet of paper. As you are doing this, note which areas you remember the least. Whether you are working with notes or the daily log, you want to discover the topics the teacher devoted more time to, the sequence of the presentations, and the relationship of topics to other topics.

Now set some very specific subject-related goals. You have discovered the topics of extreme importance. You know what areas you have to concentrate on re-learning. You can now figure out how much time you need to read your notes, re-learn the material, and prepare topic-by-topic for the test. Chart a study schedule citing study goals for each study session.

Strategy and planning are important. Do not ever expect to learn everything adequately by reading your notes or a text from the beginning to the end. Instead, plan to study notes topic by topic. This integrates the knowledge about a topic. This allows you to compare two or more topics thoroughly. It will give you the needed opportunity to form a critical opinion about each topic. You should not plan to review or re-learn the night before an exam. That night should be devoted to reciting your knowledge and sleeping.

Read, re-learn, and discover test questions

You can discover what will be on the test. Is this a surprise to you? How can you possibly do it?

—Pre-read the notes the same way you pre-read a book.

—Study the notes topic by topic. Discover the most important facts and ideas. They will be tested.

—Discover which topics really could become essay questions. Write your own essay questions and prepare outlined answers.

You will definitely be tested on factual material. Learn all definitions, items in a series, and lists of things in their specific order. Be able to visualize them in your notes. Employ any of the self-testing devices in chapter one, but concentrate on mastering the material and testing your memory. The time to organize your notes has long passed. This doesn't mean you can panic. It means you must concentrate all your efforts to re-learning the information as quickly and as thoroughly as possible.

How to prepare for essay tests

If you are going to have an essay test, try to discover the essay questions. After the topic-by-topic review, think about what you have learned. Ask yourself:

— Are there any topics full of information that can be explained? If so, refer to the informational vocabulary test list and write an informational essay question. All of the information to answer the question should be included in the thesis statement you could write to answer the question.

— Are there topics that involve character studies or descriptions? Can they be compared or contrasted? Write one or more descriptive essay questions.

— Are there topics that you could analyze and state an opinion about? Is there any relationship at all between two or more of these topics? Look at the explanatory essay vocabulary list and write an explanatory essay question.

— Can you possibly think of a question that would tie together all or several of the topics you have been studying? This would probably be a major explanatory question. Write that question. It is probably the most important one.

Now prepare an outline for each of the essay questions that you have written. Your questions should be analytical, forcing you to provide all the information that deals with the topic. Review the topic again from your notes. Are you still sure that might be the question? Does your outline include all the important information? For each essay, write a good thesis statement for the introductory paragraph. Outline the essay briefly. You only need complete sentences for the thesis statement. Learn the outline. Be able to rewrite each outline from memory. You are now fully prepared for the essay test.

The key to success: analyze the course material

Learning course content is extremely important, but analyzing what you have learned is vital for test preparation. This is exactly the process a teacher goes through in writing an exam. You can review the material and learn it, then form your opinion about the topics presented. You can analyze the course, a step that very few students even think about doing. Teachers certainly don't teach students how to write tests, but they analyze material to write them. You can discover the techniques yourself.

You can actually discover what will be on the test if you plan your study time well. The process is a very valuable one. It takes a little time, but that is extremely valuable time. You will be able to study efficiently and do very well on any test by analyzing the material you have learned.

CHAPTER 7
How to
Take Tests
Strategically

Knowing how to take a test is as important as knowing the subject matter. Know how to make a test really work for you! Your grade is a measurement of your test-taking knowledge and your memory.

You are now totally familiar with the different types of tests, vocabulary used on tests, and exam preparation techniques. Now we can bring all the ideas together to see how you can use them to ace an exam.

Read the entire test to know what you have to do

Your very first goal when you get an exam is to find out what is expected of you. Read the entire exam quickly! Do not write anything before reading it.

Incidentally, this writer administered an exam once that instructed students to write their name at the top and read the entire test. Questions followed. Several students answered the questions immediately. Students who read the whole test, as instructed, found a statement at the end that looked like a question. It instructed them to do nothing on the test except for writing their name at the top of the page. More than eighty percent of the class

47

failed. The lesson to be learned:

Read all instructions and every essay question before you do any-thing else! Find out:

1.   Precisely what you have to do:
     —What types of test questions are included?
     —Do you have to do all of the questions?
     —Does the test have to be done in any particular order?
     —Do you get more credit on one section or one essay?
     —Are there any internal clues?
     —Are there any two-part questions? Underline those instruc-
       tions.

2.   The length of the exam.
     —Is one section going to be more difficult or time consuming?
     —How much time do you have to complete the exam?

Then: Plan your strategy and allocate your time.

Decide which section you should do first, which section last, and allocate time for each section of the exam. Limit your essay answers accordingly. As you start to do the exam, re-read instruc-tions before answering questions. Be sure to do all two part answers and follow directions.

Specific tips for taking each type of test

True-false tests

First read all instructions. Analyze each statement. It is not easy for a teacher to write true-false questions. It is almost impos-sible to write one without using one or more words that limit a subject.

The words on the following list generally signal that a state-ment is false. Learn the list. Whenever one of these words appears, read the sentence very carefully. Really test the validity of the statement.

Words that generally signal a false statement:

absolutely	exactly	no	rarely
all	few	none	sometimes
always	first	not	whenever
before	last	most	
every	never	occasionally	

Non-limiting words in a true-false question generally signal that a statement is true. These words are:

often	usually	on the average
some	many	

If any part of a statement is incorrect, that statement is false! This is the most important knowledge you should have about any true-false test question. All statements must be absolutely correct, totally correct, at all times, without any exceptions, for the statements to be true. Always test every word in every statement before marking your answer.

Multiple choice tests

The following steps are necessary to answering this type of test:

1. Anticipate the correct answer before you read the possible choices.
2. Look for your answer and mark it lightly.
3. Eliminate all other choices by finding a justifiable reason why each one is not correct.
4. Re-read the question and mark your correct answer.

Tips: If you must guess, eliminate responses that you know are incorrect. Then eliminate extremes since the correct answer is generally between two extremes.

Notice if one of the answers is longer, is stated in a different vocabulary, or is slightly different in form from the other choices. That is a clue that it may be the correct answer. A teacher often has difficulty writing four or five plausible choices.

Look for any other internal clues. Notice a singular verb, an "a" or "an," or any limiting words.

Vocabulary tests:

The synonym question requires you to select a word that means the same as the stated word. The technique is:
1. Anticipate the correct answer
2. Read the choices looking for your choice.
3. Eliminate the other choices and mark the correct answer.

The antonym type multiple choice test question is really two questions in one. Therefore:
1. Think of a synonym for the word.
2. Select a word that means the opposite of your synonym.

Tip: For all vocabulary tests, the answer should be in the same grammatical form as the given word. Any word in the list of choices that is a different grammatical form is most assuredly an incorrect answer.

Analogy tests

The analogy question requires a comparison of one relationship between two objects or ideas, to another very similar relationship between two other objects or ideas. The usual form is "this is to that" as "something is to something else." These questions require several thought processes.
1. Find and state the relationship, similarity, or the dissimilarity between the first two objects or ideas.
2. Analyze the answer list. State the relationship for each possible answer and choose the set that has the same

relationship as the given set.

Proverbs are a type of analogy test. When you encounter them, think of the meaning of the first proverb, then look for another that has the same meaning.

Fill in short answer tests

Notice clues such as a singular or plural verb, an "a" or "an" preceding the writing space, or the number of lines supplied for you to write on. These generally are the only clues since you must supply the facts.

Read the questions carefully. If you have to list a number of facts, do they have to be in any particular order? Do you have to do something with the list after you have written it? Valuable points can be forfeited by not following the directions completely and accurately.

Matching tests

Pencil in the answers you are certain of first, crossing off items used on the second list as soon as they are used. Look for terminology, verb tenses, and vocabulary clues. Often you will find some that will help you.

Cross out tests

Your only approach can be to decide what is happening in the series. Next locate the response that does not fit the pattern and cross it out.

Essay tests

First determine how much total time you have for each essay. Use one fifth of that time to plan your essay and outline it. Only four fifths of the time is actually spent writing.

If the essays do not have to be done in a specific order, do the easiest one first and quickly, and the hardest one last. Lock in a good grade on the one you are fully prepared for.

If two essays are on the same topic, note how they are different. One will probably be descriptive or informative, and the other explanatory. Plan carefully and cross reference if possible.

If you must forfeit points, do the hardest essay last, but plan to spend extra time on it. Start with a good thesis statement and use your best persuasive essay writing skills.

Before writing, read the essay question, noting the terminology. Be sure to plan an answer that responds directly to the question and answers all parts of it. Mentally, or on scrap paper, list the information you need to include. Determine the all-important thesis statement. Test the thesis quickly to determine its validity and the length of the essay. Outline in the margins, on the test, or on scrap paper. Write to follow the outline so you will not stray from the subject.

Select your topic, formulate your thesis statement and get right to the point. Use simple sentences and brevity to show you have a vivid, precise knowledge of the material. You do not need to fill a blue book generally to explain your thesis.

Write as if the reader has no knowledge of the ideas you are presenting. Your teacher will not guess you have the knowledge; you must show that you do in your essay.

Use good essay style. Adapt it to fit the length of your essay. Write an introduction and include your thesis statement last. Develop each part of the thesis in subsequent paragraphs. Include a brief conclusion. Give your opinion for explanatory essays and cite reasons or substantiating evidence.

Illustrate clearly. You might include diagrams, a graph, technical terms, and a few underlined sections or words. They all indicate to a teacher that you really know the material and can clearly illustrate it. Use these devices whenever they are most appropriate, but not to excess. The key is that illustrations must be appropriate.

If you run out of time, submit a complete outline. Use concise, complete sentences. Often you may receive full credit if the outline starts with a good thesis statement, answers the questions, and is complete. Include your opinion if necessary.

If time permits, read your essays to see if you have included all the information. Correct any mis-spellings, check punctuation, and catch any careless errors you may have made.

How to make every test your greatest learning tool

What good is all the information you have learned if the test is your only means of proving it, and you have goofed? Analyze all returned tests! Don't throw them away!

Go over the returned tests and read them very carefully. See if any limiting words tripped you up in the true-false tests. See if your errors were just careless ones. See if you really answered the questions directly and followed all directions.

Analyze your essays. Perhaps you made a "list" when you were asked to "explain," or "compared" when you were asked to "contrast." Maybe you wrote a long, very detailed answer when you only needed to "state the main ideas." Perhaps you didn't state your opinion, so you lost a few precious points. Learn something from every essay. Try to improve your essay writing techniques before the next exam.

By studying returned tests and analyzing your study habits, you can improve your skills. Prepare yourself to ace the next exam. Luck is not a factor — skill is!

CHAPTER 8
Concluding Remarks
for Your
Successful Future

As we approach the end of this exploration into the study process, we can identify *five strategies applicable to the pursuit of your academic success.*

First, *decide that you will be successful.* Be your own best friend and best critic. You compete with yourself anyway. Everybody does. Have a lot of confidence in yourself. You can pull yourself up when you are down. You can maintain good study habits even when your grades are good. If you fail at something, analyze it very briefly, then let it go, and decide to move on to more successful study methods, more intensive concentration, and more frequent reviews.

Second, *establish a good basic study schedule and adapt it to fulfill all of your study requirements.* Take all possible steps to make learning as easy, productive, and complete as possible. Identify what has to be learned, plan study time, and include enough time to completely master it. With adequate planning, you won't have to spend all of your time at the books, skip a meal, or lose any sleep.

Third, *discover the teacher's lesson plan.* Write class assignment logs every day. Take good notes. Analyze and criticize the material topic by topic. Review and re-learn frequently. Discover what will be on the exams and start preparing for tests several days in advance.

Fourth, *know as much as possible about the various types of tests.* Master the terminology involved so you can make every test situation work for you.

Fifth, *take charge of your life as a student!* Don't let the courses control you. You control them! Organize your time and the materials so you accomplish what you have to learn in a limited period of time. Make the time you spend on any project and every assignment very productive learning time. Have fun too. Try to create a balance between studies and pleasure.

You can be a very successful student. Set your goals high and work to achieve them. It only takes a little determination and conscientious planning on your part. It only takes a little effort. Luck is not a factor, but good luck in your pursuit of excellence.

GLOSSARY

Words and Concepts You Will Use

analyze	to break down into various parts, present an opinion, and draw some conclusions
apply	to use knowledge practically and specifically, sometimes in relationship to new material
argue	to state conclusive evidence, reasons for and/or against. Same meaning as "discuss" and "debate"
cite	to quote a passage, book, speech, or writer; to give examples, proof or explanation; or to name a person, place, or thing
characterize	to describe the particular qualities, features, or traits of a person or group
choose	to select
clarify	to state the meaning precisely showing the distinguishing characteristics
classify	to arrange, rank, or group according to a system or characteristics
compare	to examine the qualities or characteristics, then

	show their similarities and/or differences
contrast	same as "compare" but show only the differences or dissimilarities
criticism	a verbally expressed act of evaluation and assessment
criticize	to examine a subject, give your judgment or opinion, and state "why" you arrived at your conclusion
daily log	a separate section in your notebook listing in one column the assignments and information about them, and in another column, the main topics presented in class
decide	to pass judgment, argue, or reach a decision
demonstrate	to prove, explain using examples, show and clarify including reasons to support the proof
depict	to portray or picture in words
describe	to tell about, giving a very detailed account
descriptive essay	an essay that conveys the writer's dominant impression of a topic
differentiate	to show the special differences or dissimilarities
discuss	to examine a subject from all angles, to clarify by stating evidence and reasons for and/or against. Same as argue and review
enumerate	to list or name without further elaboration, unless the instructions tell you to do something else with the list as well
essay	a three-part composition that has an introduction that presents the writer's topic and what is going to be said about that topic (thesis statement), a body that develops each part of the thesis, and a conclusion that summarizes the

ideas and briefly explains their significance

explanatory essay	an essay in which the writer evaluates a subject, states his opinion, and substantiates that opinion
evaluate	to appraise, to find and describe the value or worth of an idea
expand	to develop an idea or topic in detail. In math: to develop the entire equation step-by-step
exemplify	to explain and clarify by giving examples or comparisons
give	to state or name
how	to fully explain, give a reason, intent, purpose, or the effect of
identify	to name a thing that has identical or the same characteristics, or can be treated the same as something else. Frequently used in place of to "name" or "list"
illustrate	to explain and clarify by giving examples or comparisons. Same as "exemplify"
informational essay	an essay that reveals facts about a topic
list	to name
name	to state or list
narrate	to tell in writing, give an account of what is happening, to recount, to relate
organize	to arrange, establish a list, or to write an outline
outline	note-taking form stating the main topic in a complete sentence and indenting for sub-topics
prove	to fully establish the validity or truth, to

	demonstrate a fact. In math: to test or verify a calculation
quote	to repeat a passage verbatim
recall	to remember and describe, list or name
recount	to relate or narrate, to give a detailed account of, in order, if necessary
relate	same as narrate and recount
review	to examine a subject from all angles, to clarify by stating evidence and the reasons for and/or against. Same as discuss and argue on essays
select	to choose, generally for its specific quality or characteristic that you will relate
show	to point out, clarify, demonstrate, explain
sketch	to give a brief plan or description of main points or parts, or to outline briefly
state	to name or list
study	the act or process of applying the mind to acquire knowledge. Note: "process" means critical examination of subject matter
substantiate	to show the truth or reality by giving evidence, facts, and proof
summarize	to give a condensed outline of main points, omitting minor details
synthesize	to bring together a whole idea by integrating its parts. In philosophy: to arrive at deductive reasoning from simple thoughts to complex ideas, explaining the cause and effect, noting the principle, and how it applies
tell	same as narrate, enumerate, recount, list, or it could mean to relate in order, to express in words, give an account of, or give evidence of

thesis statement	a two-part generalization statement that is a precise statement of the subject of the essay. The predicate of the statement tells what the writer is going to say about that subject
trace	to write the development, process, or history of something in sequence, or to draw a diagram or graph
what	to identify, qualify, or give a quantity. Often "what" is used to ask about the value, importance, or the effect of something
when	to state an occurrence or occasion